all these urban fields

by loisa fenichell

ISBN 978-1-733951-50-0

Cover by Ericka Longo
Cover Photograph by Loisa Fenichell
All Photographs by Loisa Fenichell

Typeset in Spectral
Designed with Free software, including LibreOffice

Published by Nothing to Say, Inc.
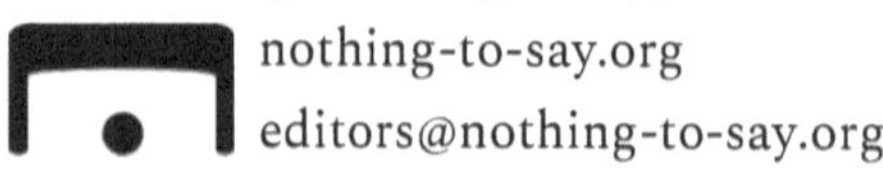
nothing-to-say.org
editors@nothing-to-say.org

For those who analyze. For those who eloquently love. For the teachers: Monica Ferrell; Kathleen McCormick; Anthony Domestico; Gaura Narayan; Lee Schlesinger. For cities. For farmscapes. For dogs and cats alike.

While most of these poems are new to the world at large, 'birth' has been published in Pink Monkey Magazine, *'inconsistencies' in Purchase College's literary magazine* Italics Mine, *and 'when I said I was pious what I meant was' in Purchase College's alternative literary magazine* Submissions Magazine.

I

AS PROLOGUE

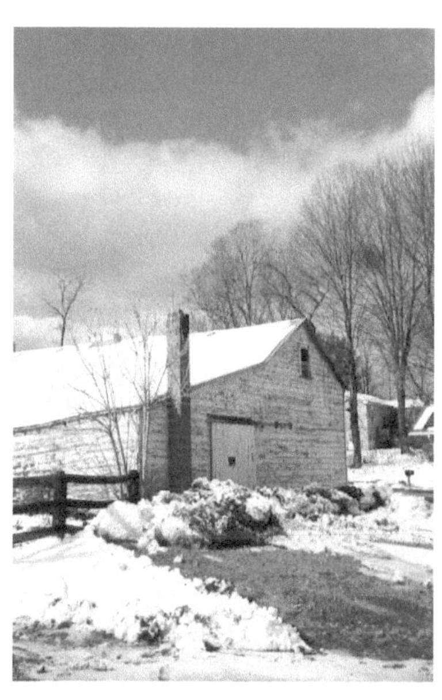

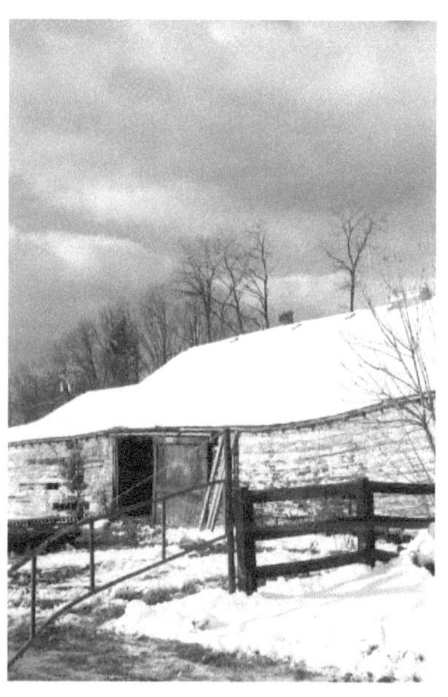

a will to live

mountain range
oilscape
stovetop
campsite
scrambled eggs
scraped bears
he does not return
he returns he returns he returns he returns
he returns he returns he returns he re
he returns
he returns
he returns he
when the peak hashes the sky
am inside of my wrists like Sunday's door frame
barefoot, my eyes cursed out
by nobody new

housewarming

I behaved
I gutted myself

I was to you
spatial practice

Nauseating it was when you
held my chin up
for all the garish light to see

steady

motley times of yearning
amidst atomization of crueler buildings

I cobble together life:

pancake houses, all hours of the night;
fires from which neither of us receive
our true incinerations.

fires' dearest lights creep through my stomach
like proper rashes. these dearest lights
remain for your face to clutch.

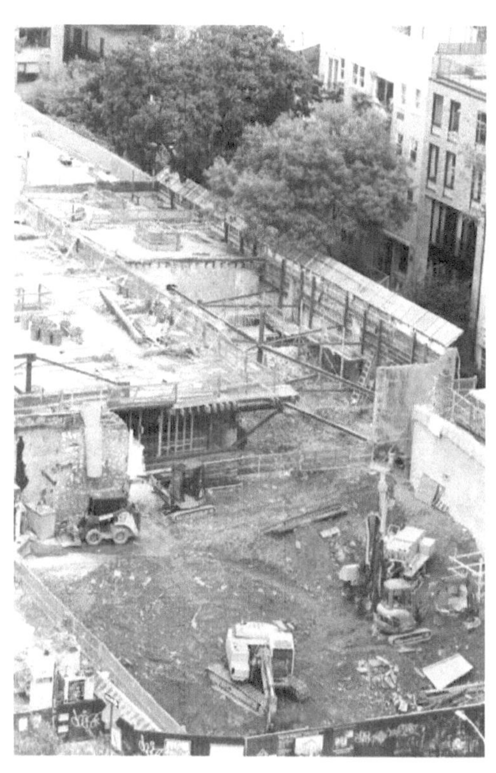

II

AS INFANT

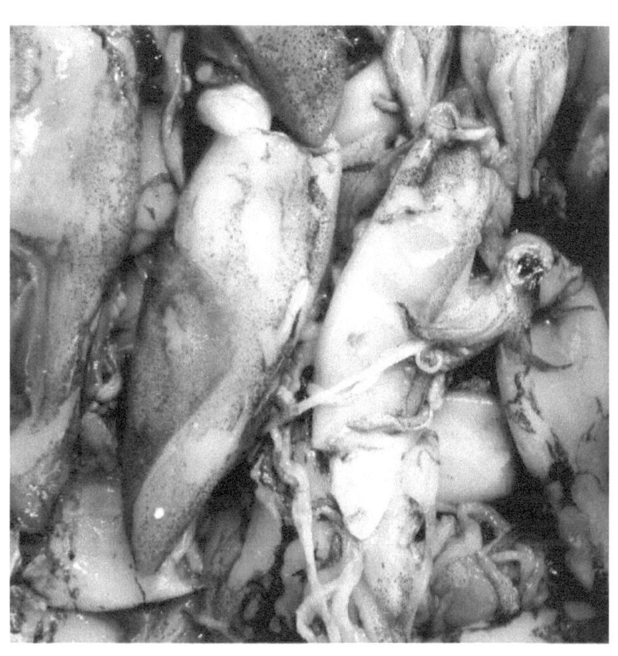

birth

Anne is all mirrors: a
contemporary girl, youth & born
into complacency! She

obsesses best when she
cannot keep a secret: also known as
the propensity for the more dramatic
kinds of lighting: also, on stage she breaks

like a recurring nightmare.
Though when asked, she does not dream.
When asked, she would prefer
to wear large paper pink bags
as dresses & suck in her stomach
until it dissolves like chicken
feathers—these she does not collect.

She bears no collections to her name

& she does not dream.

She does not see—
that upon her birth
she lay in the hospital
& the nurses called her 'o beauty,
beauty!' but she keeps her beauty

to herself, driven deeply into her chest
like seas of uncleanliness.

inconsistencies

Let me writhe on pavement ripped
by sun. Rumor has it that that's how
my mother was born.

Rumor has it that that's how I was born, too.
I picture my birth the way I picture the bible,
happening between two gentle and soft fingertips.
Reverent whispers, because, not to brag,
but I was the first child. The first child,
the hardest child.

I like to think that it stormed that night.
That the rumors are wrong.
That I wasn't born in the sun.
That the night of my birth, the electricity went out,
& my parents were left without light.

I like to think that they wept when I was born.
That they wept again when they could finally turn on a lamp,
& watch its sparks burst the way I did from the womb.

flyover myth

Saw my beauty once, briefly,
like a flyover myth. My skin chilled
& I ate with a vengeance
as though curled into the smallness of a child's lap.
I could have been—once was—this child,
which I found appealing like the breaking open
of a new country into dizziness.

Back then it was every night
that the dizziness tasted across my wish
for a paler belly. I didn't know how to stop
the endless consummation or the breaking
of the small bones of my swollen ankles.

There had been a love that had swelled,
then stitched apart, between us,
like the growing confusion of my own
hardly kept secret genre of hunger.
Back then, instead of sleeping, I walked through
blank hallways & pictured myself limping
through gardens flowered in when you took
my first virginity. It was with you I slept,
atop a bed of white sheets like fish scales.
I spent a week after that disturbingly awake
in my own bed, convinced each time I looked down
that the comforter atop my stomach
was just another layer of fat. At the time
this was all I could reduce myself to:
strata of fat & dehydrated cells.

candle story

i.

I write this for you, the reader—

my father is not yet dead   yet still I am at
somebody's funeral!
yours, perhaps—& yet it is not even winter!

by the time you read this   your body will be bruised
it will be both of our birthdays
we will be on an airplane
there will be candles
they will be too bright
for the pilot to fly

ii.

candles squeezed into
the mouth of the pilot
like a murder spell

once it came time
for our legs to break
at the seams of laughter
it was time for us
to clap our hands—

iii.

to you, only to you, do I tell
of my weaknesses: the spot of laughter
in the weak spot of sun
remains sin unto itself

then, too, that my birth within these pages
came within the softness of only your voice!

my parents, at my birth, dubbed me '*weak talent*
like ginger tea!' at my birth each felt nausea crash
into them like broken airplanes   it was in a motel
my mother sprawled across the bathtub as though
her legs were broken   in the corner of the room
lay the dog, bruised & mewling, watching me
like a fixation onto Jesus Christ   I never did fall like webbed hands
into Christianity

but when as an infant I rolled onto my soft stomach
I felt immediately an illness like a plague of fields
gone without any style of reaping—   my other weakness:
at any mention
of rape, I fainted, cinema-style, bruised at the knees

carry me well, reader, I will be yours!

iv.

when we run together I will be jealous
though we will keep at the same pace

v.

my other origin story
came from my knuckles: I only know you, reader, when I am
injured! my mother in her mouth suckled at the tree branches
I cut into just for her. my best option for narrative
was always that though I could not run I could marry.

I was 13 when the pauper transformed me in the rhythm
of quick candles into a majesty—to the wrists did I take
one of these candles, then paused, still
as a cadaverous white rhinoceros
in my tracks: interminable violence, you are not yet a world war

but still with you, dear reader, am I willing to start
a movement!

vi.

like a candle stuffed within the mouth I gnawed
at my tongue until the taste of sun came out
to bounce atop my legs   it was the morning
I was not sad   alternate narrative:

back in the motel room
I learned finally to hide in the bathtub (with my mother)—
to pretend, interminably, to be taking a bath

martyr me

In the darkness my voice spread, eagle-like, frightened—scared,
as desert storm—I was
curled up not very much besides you   I was

all brown-eyed chambermaid, chamber pot resting carefully
underneath my bed, tin buckets resting above my head
like a soldier's bloodied theatre spell. The best
kind of theatre is when you are finally here,
besides me

where the snakes rattle beneath my bookshelves

& a doll named Alice does not lose her arm. In the airport I was,
crying like the song
played on repeat   dizzied as golden thread
wept now   in a garden
drizzled next   screwdrivered next   nuzzled in my sweater,
by my fire,

I was not

no longer afraid but

inside the river I spread
my legs wide
just for you

watched as the blood pooled like plates of arugula
pear skin
apple peel
the food I ate before soon I would
be prayed to by the shower drain

thought I knew you but I just rested besides
thought I knew you but I just dolled up named Alice did not lose

her arm
cool careful
in my throat
I am

when the no calls returned   the druggist
hidden
in the basement
arrested

he is Jewish
but he does not pray   we
are Jewish but by the Eastern Parkway
we do not sit

the brother culled forth the false prayers

(he clawed at my face;
left no scratches)

the december in which he
finally pulled the shotgun
only the horse heard; the cows;
the dead lion (did not exist).

we had the same scorched bone.

by the river, the moss hymned forward.
we chewed at the staleness.
the foxes chewed at their wires.

command discussion

Talk of moon, bloody! Count chickens
during breakfast period. Bring to light
that my mother was always cruel, always wet.

Bracket off the paved world in which brother
& I now live. Make heavy, make high that,
when younger, we popped red balloons

for the savior. It all went something like this:
eating dragon fruit by the lake, smelling
the coolness of the pines, the water's warmth.

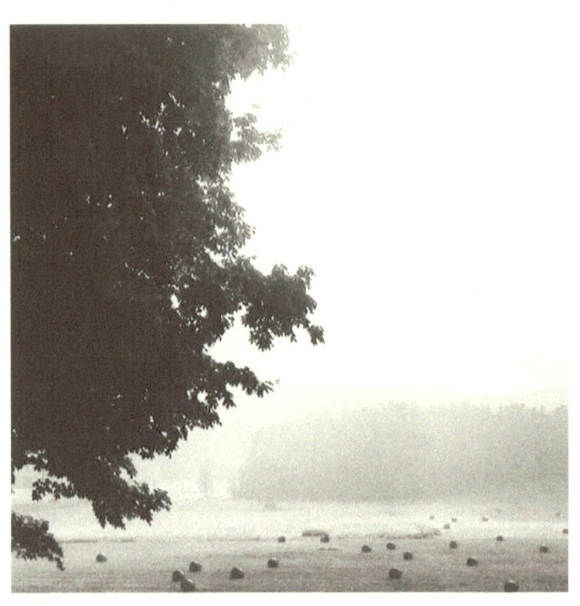

grandmother's apartment

Remaining constant in a state of terror
breaks down walls. Jesus hangs upon a wall
& I break down. In a dream I conjure up
when sleeping in my grandmother's bed
every man wears a white shirt & has blue bones.

Upon awakening my initial reaction is to stand
in the kitchen & allow the kind of light that can come
only in the mornings—somewhere in between drab
& gaudy, like a drove of bright bees—to percolate
through the window above the sink & press hard
against the back of my hands as I scrub them
savagely underneath running pasty tap water.

I want to eat the honeydew from my grandmother's
fridge, let the juice dribble over the floor, the tops
of my feet. It is not that I do not love my grandmother
but that when, finally, she does die, I will be unable
to view her death as anything more than happenstance.

III

AS ROMANCE

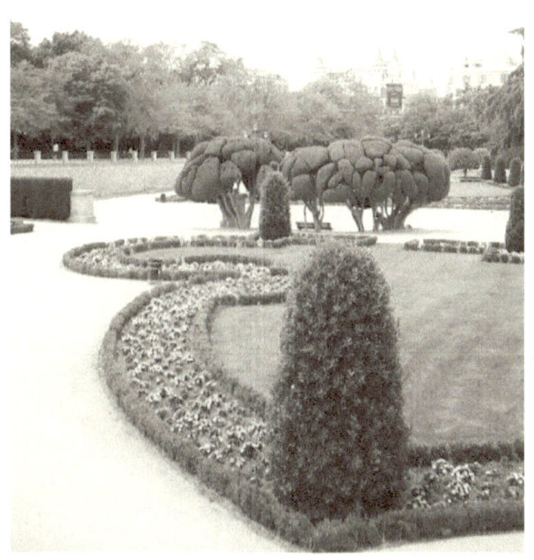

country song for the ages

Doll-sit, cold, this blue gown is all for—kill the man.
Crave the beast. Hunt the wild. Sinner-boy comes calling
for me to go forth like a bellied-bear. Nothing haunts him.
He sits pissed upon his haunches, drinks nothing but milk.
Mother wishes to murder him with her stained hands.

I am dragon-infested, slumber-eyed, lake-sat
amidst the cooled moss. Sinner-boy, I have undone the gown
while the moss still cools like rockcliff.
The lake still arrives unraveled. Consider our own romance
is linear as stomachache. Virus of the throat
reminds me that dead bitch is still surrounded by flies.

She was my bitch: a good dog does good deeds.
Consider I am on my way to you carriage-style: so very good.

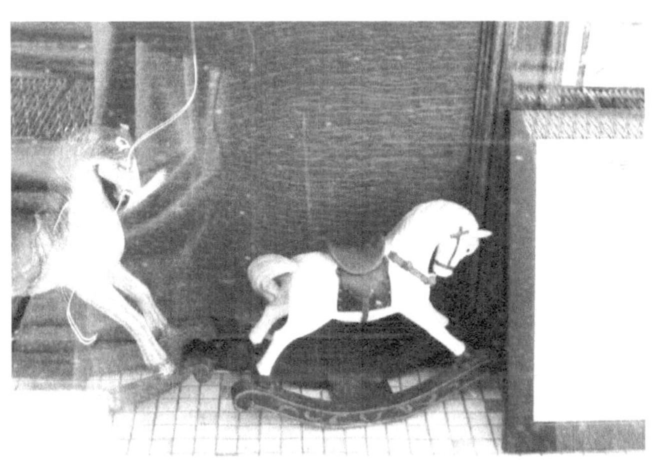

true ecstasy

I saw him laughing, once: a purple
balloon, & water, for the changes.

The lake came to call—I was sick
with all that was lavender, all coolness—

illness was stitched into my sides like streams
of cotton. He died, once in misery, once,

in yellow teeth. He never could tell me
to dance. Never could inform me of when,

truly, I, amidst high peaks, beered open
my gums. Cut apart my fingers! He will

find me there with the sweetest of sea-
gulls. Find me with the infected; I am his.

call & response

Bird's bloody sill.
Still, diving—to seas;
to mist: your lust
to carry now.

We stayed
in no motel.
Bird cawed
to no waste.

his name was Benjamin & I loved him

Savior sits watching me like my doll who roams
free as silt past my window. The whole of us
have turned balloons! God please I have turned
to knife!

Whooping coughs now turn me to sainthood.
Reliable I am, little birds, & ladies riding horses
through the park. We are all ladies here, Mother,
& the boy who cries for his crops & itches his ear
fastidiously. Mother, change your tune! Your eyeballs

drift in & out of their lids like saltmaids. The two of us
have eaten this salt for days—good of company this salt
has been for us! Providing the extra skin that folds down
like the boy's hands over my lower abdomen, how he
whispers & how he itches! "Lover please come to me

—be a dear; dog-ear me now!"

december

All night I have wanted your goldfinch.
All night I have wanted your goldfinch.
All night I have wanted your goldfinch.

there's no one I'd rather be with

But on the eve of some great moontalk
I am shivering 'neath it all like the roofs
that tremble come summer heat. Only
it is winter, still, & it is Maine within the pine
that I seek, & great gallons brimmed with salt.

I am not Lot! But still sexual relations have long
been compromised by bloody sills, by seals gone
to waste. I am—what!—a thing to be. Sculpture
I am not; never could have been with you there
on that train. I knew of love gone in rhythms
of the tomato plant; of the bells that rang; I slept!

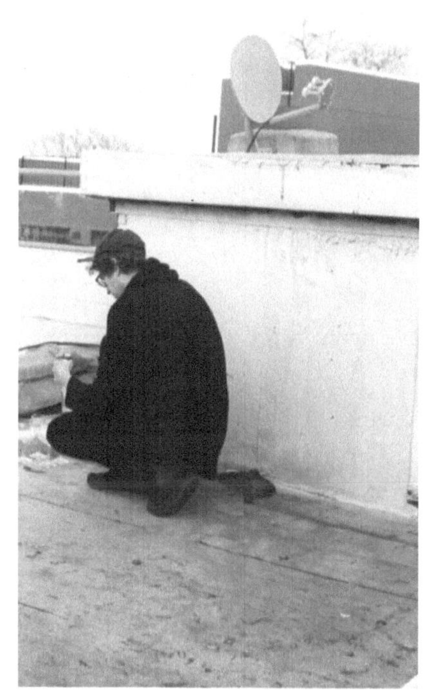

about the state

the waters rushed towards us like biblical storytime!
we were identical in our woodry! we were intending to cast
some sort of system!
we meant for you to be the old dog perched atop my damp clothes!

the sky curated the evergreens.
we dreamt up then that these trees had become
unholy; sacristy untended to in these wooded parks.
(recreational romance. rooted within simultaneous time & location.)

i did want in a particular fashion: to be enveloped by your bandits;
to waltz when i ought to have run. o, rabbit! run away; run

away away away away away away away away away   away
                              a way
(in which we have been)

dismembered, severed by banks of water. i still want!

your hand clasps mine! i feel now

steady.

coruscating

It was when we harvested the sheets of your bed
made me think we would always be blue
& wholly within the Atlantic waters.

I taught myself to swim, only   wore a scarf
for seascapes
          tight around my neck like the lungs slain afloat
          in my womb.

          Once in the future

we could have waded about your bedroom; built atop
your floor a small pool in which to flay & flail like elderly maids.

I thought often of the whale-in-miniature
tattooed across your otherwise barren chest;
the cunningness with which you
left your bedroom lights turned on throughout the night.

The night I near left your bed piss-stained
I had never seen you so fatherly; so   (luminescent!)   I
have heard tell

the earth as many: as prodigious: as demure: foreign beast
          best for grappling with the shore; with the dead fathers, each
          one of them corpses lined up along your bedroom wall. O

but we yearn for the best dead mothers! We need for them
to parenthesize us like snakes. I hated the snake! He whistled
in your room
while you slept; I had never felt so   awake:
          fear that the dragon would take you away.

for safekeeping

i.

interest me, in me, lost woman amongst the garden cubes.
the fire that, finally, really burned, in real time—our home
in maine drowned under the saint george river.   yes I

tore the body

that we wanted

plucked the weeds we wetted
(the bare chests)

when the bears crawled, at night, to our bed (burned),
we made it out alive because we were not yet sleeping.

it was alright because you—gosh—held my hand

ii.

to find that I am
direction West.

to see that I am taking you
with me
(in our scrupulous car)

in the canyon we sang out the melodies. what we missed. blankets.
dried throats. the hermits within us could live (these dead men
missed us, like the police with their bullets—

made it out

iii.

alive) fishing. ended up in alaska where it was cold because sin
was weather because I
liked you. you held my hand. both of us afraid to say:

love was like how our dog was only thirsty. how we had not had
water in three years.

iv.

I am constructing a world in which you forgive me like the tortoise:
for when I spilled
wine on your sheets; did not take the subway to greet you
where the planes landed like grand combs of teeth.
nights grew late so I

stroked your teeth. still: silence (I have always been bade—by you—
to speak away my silence!) where the only verb I know
ought to have been.

v.

to here: still unknown! that I am in a bathtub. that this new house will too one day freeze over before hell can even come into consideration. consider this: I liked the river sand the best, then the snow in alaska, now the dirt that we trail like roaches onto the carpet each day it rains (everyday). we have yet to live in the city. still I imagine the lights there to be like that which shines from the corpse of the first dog we ever owned.

vi.

here is to the dog days! clinks shared between our two glasses.
it is not that I enjoy the taste of wine,
though with you—

hello!

if you say this is done in the park at sunlight

I will hold up my quarters for when strangers stay inside
of their houses, for when I dress robe-like & sin

say there has been another call for the pigeons
who peck death-style at the hotdogs of the passerby
say in the playground the swings are made of wood

my children will ride along them each day
they will not know how to curse

or that within their father's land there is a plane up above

it is the plane that unites us like plastic spoons

then say that I am your only lover, & yours,   say that my
parents, when they met, died in a cab
the brooklyn street lamps could not mourn

even now the bridge stretches taut over the park,
& the subway makes loud
as the neighbors who together in their bedroom seem unlike what we
have made out of our own twin beds

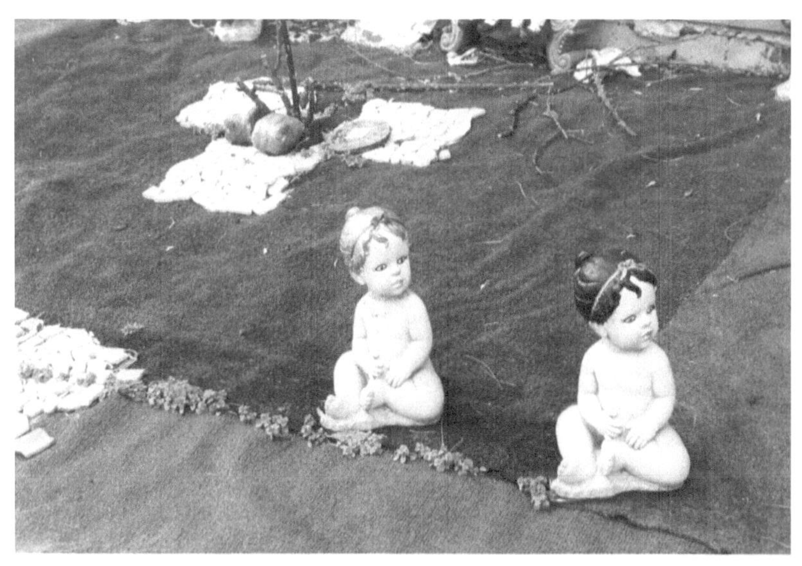

cloisters

Inside of the stone apartment, we carve out plates of arugula
for breakfast:

a single fried egg. You are finished with the famished.
Chicken feathers singe above the lack of mantelpiece
like suicidal offerings.

To the cloisters we drive like bits of dried up pear peel
(those bits still appear in my vomit days later). Three water bottles

on the dashboard. Each one of them is empty. My friend! My god

fits best within your head now! (This is middle school dance
style, with bloody teeth hanging from the children's torsos. My
children,

my friend, will not know how to spell "witchcraft.") In a diner
we pause like narrative spillage. The waitress tells us of her most

recent miscarriage. This is Washington Heights style, cinematic,
we are reeling from the deaths of the cockroaches
that died on our own bodies.

my apologies

You translate me better than any language ever could.
          Make me better.   Make it out
alive, like the dead owlets' eyes
that are clasped between my hands like prayer.
We went camping   like wenches,   glistening
fingertips,   country wild like her blue skirt still
hidden within the folds
of your head. Say: this was when my name
was forgotten. Say: this: when I
spread open the bottle of water, then wine, then you, went walking,
three miles Magellan-style around the circumference of the lake.
          Forgive me:
it is your desire to own the cats who mewl lakeside that I want;
your need for townsmen, for township.

Wild countryside, I do love you! Better than any man
could ever have held me. I am singed amongst the dirt
& rocks like how the rain brings
about the flood finally when I least expect it,
& the world in its entirety
is cancelled. Forgive me! You & your cats have been cancelled.
Forgive me!
For when you hid her hair around the corners of the tent,
forgetting to cut mine own.
It's your silliness I want when you
down your glass of beer
in a single gulp. Your hands smell of seaweed & dead gilded fish,
so perhaps I do love.

Forgive!

Little words yours tonight.
Little pigeons. Little doggies,
oversized jumpsuits, hopping
in dearest dreams around my head.

I intend to sleep tonight, even
in this state of "nausea."

Even with the mirror, juts out of the walls
like carbon dioxide. My stomach yours tonight.

I hold the small towns we never visited.
Though my hands are busy. Though my hands.
Though my hands are busy. Even the bees,
they have come to stay.

when I said I was pious what I meant was

pious for you.

We stand on rocks
& I scrape my knees.
Is this what it means to feel closer
to a god?
It's that blood, how it oozes out
like dead rivers.

How could I have forgiven you
for all that you did for me
when I asked you specifically
for nothing?

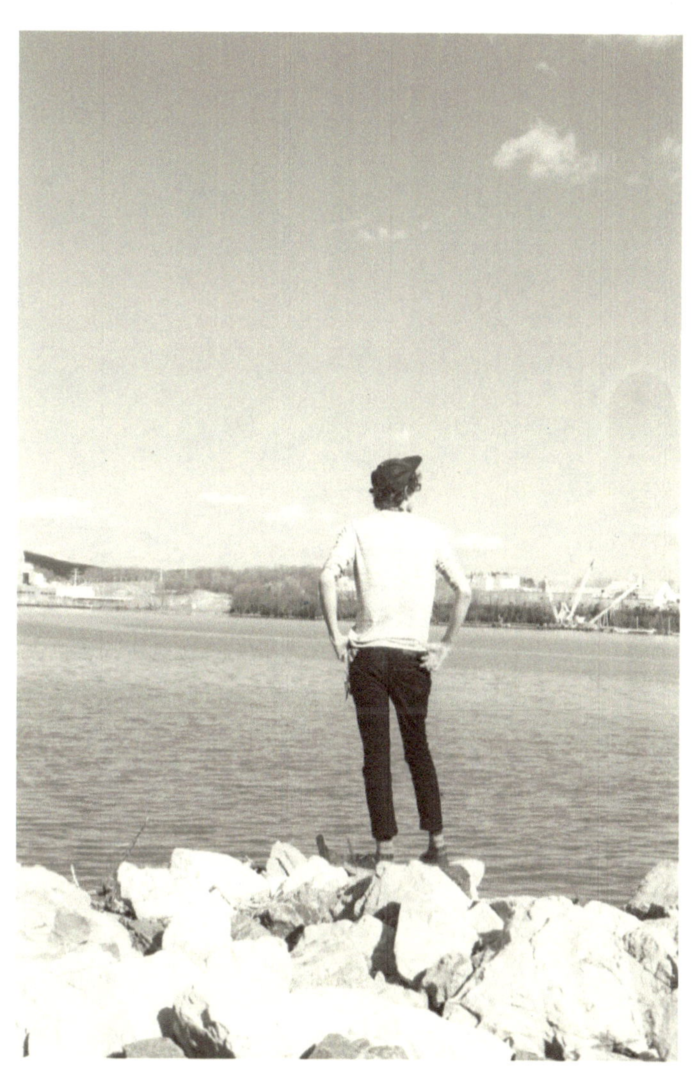

AS ENDING

What we do know: a boy gave her a pillow, sold it to her for 5 dollars, then asked if they could just be friends. She asks, what does this mean? We say, we do not know. She says, who lives in the house with him? One pillow, which he's sold to her, 3 cats, a poster of a French girl. (Alternatively, he gave her a cigarette, then told her to, 'fuck off.')

about the author

Loisa Fenichell is into rooftops, and balconies, and finding warmth wherever she can in the rather strange metropolis (NYC) she now finds herself living in. She attended SUNY Purchase, where she studied Creative Writing and Literature. Her work can be found in various publications, both online and in print, such as Winter Tangerine Review, Electric Cereal, The Rising Phoenix, Boston Accent Lit, Gandy Dancer, Italics Mine, Pink Monkey Magazine, Bottlecap Press (online blog), and Porridge Magazine.

www.ingramcontent.com/pod-product-compliance
Lightning Source LLC
LaVergne TN
LVHW050946080826
845145LV00004B/1433

* 9 7 8 1 7 3 3 9 5 1 5 0 0 *